DR ZEEMAN'S CATASTROPHE MACHINE

MARTIN FIGURA

INDEPENDENT INNOVATIVE INTERNATIONAL

Published by Cinnamon Press
Meirion House
Tanygrisiau
Blaenau Ffestiniog
Gwynedd, LL41 3SU
www.cinnamonpress.com

The right of Martin Figura to be identified as author of this work
has been asserted by him in accordance with the Copyright,
Designs and Patent Act, 1988. Copyright © 2015 Martin Figura.
ISBN:978-1-910836-18-7
British Library Cataloguing in Publication Data. A CIP record for
this book can be obtained from the British Library.

Designed and typeset in Palatino by Cinnamon Press. Printed in
Poland

Original cover design by Adam Craig.

Cinnamon Press is represented in the UK by Inpress Ltd
www.inpressbooks.co.uk and in Wales by the Welsh Books
Council www.cllc.org.uk

Acknowledgements

Thanks to the the following where some of the poems have been published or performed:
Border: *Sculpted, Poetry of the North West* edited by Lindsey Holland and Angela Topping; Brogues: Shoes or no Shoes Museum; Paradise Street: *'More Raw Material: work inspired by Alan Sillitoe,* edited by Neil Fulwood & David Sillitoe (Lucifer Press, 2015); Reservist: *Wenlock Poetry Fesitval Anthology* 2012; To A Grey Seal: *Shortlisted in The Rialto* Nature Poetry Competition 2015; *The Interpreter's House*; Rooks: *King's Lynn Silver Folio Anthology* ed Michael Hulse & performed as part of The Voice Project's Ideas of Flight at the Norfolk & Norwich Festival 2013; School Room, Upper Silesia 1933: *The Rialto* & Commended in The Ledbury Festival Poetry Competition; *Ink, Sweat & Tears;* Sensing Space: Sensing Spaces, Wandering Words *Ekphrasis at the RA;* The King James Version: Commended in The Ledbury Festival Poetry Competition; *The Interpreter's House;* The Machine Gun performed as part of the Voice project's Souvenir at the Norfolk & Norwich Festival 2014.

And to the editors of the following magazines for publishing versions of:
Sugar: *Iota;* Bird: *London Grip;* Dr Zeeman's Catastrophe Machine: *Magma;* Ears: *Iota;* The Difference Machine: *Iota;* How to Make a Family: *Magma;* The Bonsack Machine: *The Interpreter's House;* Reservoir: *Magma;* Coat: *Peony Moon;* The Life Support Machine: *The Interpreter's House;* Washing Machine: *Paris Lit Up;* Fixed: *Fat Damsel;* Grain: *Fat Damsel – Take Ten Section;* Amy's Lovers: *Prole;* Calendar; *Prole.*

I owe huge thanks to our workshop group of: Esther Morgan, Matthew Howard, Joanna Guthrie, Jonathan Morley, Tiffany Atkinson, Andrea Holland, Andy McDonnell and Helen Ivory, who have all helped in improving many of these poems.

And thank you to everyone who's encouraged me, especially those who've booked me to read.

Contents

For Helen, with love

Dr Zeeman's Catastrophe Machine

(René) Thom has employed the theory in an endeavour to understand how language is generated. It is an intriguing thought that the same mathematics may underlie not only the way genetic code causes the embryo to unfold but also the way the printed word causes our imagination to unfold.

Dr E.C. Zeeman *Catastrophe Theory*

Rooks

for Mark Cocker

Their broken voices call against the hard ground
of a day's work. They are the dark coming home
in dissonant scores until this field of stubble
is soft-black with them, the telephone wires
thick and bowed. Ten thousand grey tongues
honour the dusk, the Lowestoft commuter train,
the woods of Buckenham Carrs.

Thrown like muck from a wheel until the sky
is blind with them, they are the exact opposite
of stars. And here they come, all bluster,
their ostentatious flight across the moon
to the hierarchy of branches, to the rough
belonging of bark in their claws.

Brogues

Joseph Cheyney's since you ask—classic
handmade mahogany. A sale purchase
from the shop with three hundred quid
monogrammed velvet slippers in the window.

Black polish and a soft cloth mate, it antiques
the shine—this from a Deptford face with pin-sharp pupils
who's never spoken to me before, apart from that time
on the dance floor, when he barked *shift yer arse*.

Less than a year on and I can feel every little stone.
The shop ladies are polite in a certain way
and send them off to their man. They return weeks later
tissue-wrapped with a hand-written receipt.

In the cracked mirror of my room: a flash of red sock,
the sharp crease of Prince of Wales check, pockets empty
from the cost, a button-down collar and thin black tie.
Soles so slick the worn stair-carpet may as well be ice.

I stride out to rough them up a little, head up the hill
to the twitching curtains and long drives with borders
like medal ribbons, my steel quarter heels on their gravel.

Border

When he goes south, it's with a reluctant
and suspicious step, ear cocked
to the wind ready for the first trace
of a clipped accent, the first slight
to knot the muscles inside his coat.

He speaks as little as possible, just enough
to get supplies, and if asked to repeat himself
rolls the words around his mouth, spits
them out, points, as if it were obvious.

Maroon Machine

The Parachute Regiment's red beret

A shove and shout and you're out in the roar
and the next second yanked clear of the line
like a doll, and the Iron Age hummocky Plain
below, a thrown dun cloth in the afternoon glare.

Your boots are 3D and things become clear:
Old Sarum's a cup-ring, Stonehenge a broken
mouth, tank-tracks criss-crossing the chalk terrain
and its burial mounds like self-harm scars.

This place will take all the grit you possess.
Shouts from Bruneval to Al Basrah echo
the corridors, learn them by heart. This beret is all,
leave your luggage at the door, etch us
into your skin like a blood group tattoo,
fall quiet from the sky, hit the ground and roll.

Paradise Street I

Out of the Strong Came Forth Sweetness Judges 14:14

*1941 * Blitz*

The Mersey is a hungry mouth, her dark city night
torn down by bombers, her fearful people
in cellars. In the blood-red after-fire of the docks

SS Malakand's munition belly swells and explodes,
her tonnage of anchor hurled through the trembling sky
to the hospital steps. A fireman lies at the gates,

his coming-of-age watch stopped on his wrist. A lad
surfaces through diesel and puke, hands slapping
at the water, teeth chattering in his skull. The burnt

toffee stench is burning at his throat, the burning shore
so far away. A mother stumbles from the shelter,
hurries pale along Paradise Street, its pavement of rats.

She flinches in the after blast and clutches her Maggie,
her sweet baby, eyes wheels of flame. Across Bootle,
Kirkdale and Walton, the thin wail of sirens strung out for the loss.

Paradise Street II

*1953 * Shallcross Street: Red, White and Blue.*

Men smoke buttoned up and slick as if Sunday.
Women load shrouded trestle tables, the cake's
top tier askew on Doric columns. Fancy dress kids

pose dead-dog still for the Echo's photographer.
Maggie, eye-patched and one scabby knee bent, leans
on the worn head of a cut down broom, calls to her uncle:

aargh Jim Lad. Jim's Bantam splutters about, kids
bouncing in its sidecar: eggs loose in a box.
At nightfall, someone's upright piano

is lugged from their parlour out to the street.
Who wouldn't feel sentimental under such bunting,
under such stars, and fill their lungs

for *O Waly, Waly,* for *Liverpool Lullaby:*

> *Although you have no silver spoon*
> *Better days are coming soon.*

Paradise Street III

*1834 * Young Barker*

falls to his bony knees, sings
Miss Dobson a lullaby:

> *A-gath'ring flowers both red and blue,*
> *I little thought of what love can do.*

A tiny shop on Paradise Street
from their union, something sweet.

Paradise Street IV

*1963 * Barker and Dobson Sweet Factory*

Girls pour through the gates, dipper hands sticky
from putting the twist into buttered brazils. Arm
-in-arm they sway, a necklace of misshapes strung

the width of Whitefield Road singing themselves
home for Friday tea, sifting out to Everton's
furrowed brow of terraces. Below, the docks

loose flat-hatted men with thirsts more than equal
to a ten bob note. Bizzies brace for the Blue
and the Red, the Taig and the Prod. Jim has a joke,

digs deep in his pocket, puts off the stagger
up the hill until his belligerence is tight enough,
the kids asleep in bed. Maggie scrubs herself squeaky,

puts on the lippy, promises her da she'll be on
that last bus. Once safe round the corner
she hitches her skirt, lets the Devil walk her

to the top of Breck Road, show her the city
spread out brightly below. And look
at the gob on it! This Mersey mouth will spill

from transistors and Dansettes, cross oceans,
set girls screaming with a shake of its moppy head,
write a new history in sweat on cellar walls.

Maggie steadies herself at the Necropolis gates.
Is this the love everyone's singing about
or just a Tate and Lyle lorry trundling past.

Paradise Street V

*1981 * Cantril Farm*

Slum-cleared here in the Summer of Love.
One road in, no road out, no buses or pubs
or goats or pigs come to that.

At night you can hear the 'Mancs' in the safari park
or maybe it's just the motorway roaring past.
Love Lane Refinery's gone, there's no sugar left.

The Devil watches the city burn
from his tower block, and Maggie
falls out of love with her name.

Paradise Street VI

*1807 * Kitty Amelia*

Captain 'Mind your Eye' Crow sets the last slaver
against the current, her three hundred tons of burden
cleaves rough water not healing in her wake.

Paradise Street VII

*2008 * European City of Culture*

The Albert Dock all done up and Maggie's lad
Michael visiting from London—*I know the shame, the shame.*
He walks her quietly through the Maritime Museum:

the old docks' handmade bricks, wartime heroes
lost at sea, the shackles of the slave ship's hold,
the masters' commemoration, cast in iron:

>Rodney Street,
>Ashton Street,
>Sir Thomas Street
>Penny Lane.

She saw them *loads of times* down the Cavern
where her mother clutched her the night
the sky blazed and where his father told her

the first lie, a good one too, that he was
Billy Liddell's son and had a trial at Anfield, which
was almost true; the trial was not at Anfield though.

They're making over Paradise Street: Liverpool One,
Liverpool's Mayfair: apartments, leisure
facilities, bronzey goose-pimple girls

and retail outlets. John Lewis's for a treat.
He opts for the healthy option, Maggie stirs
three sugars into her tea and enjoys the view.

Paradise Street VIII

*2012 * Stockbridge Village (formerly Cantril Farm)*

Tarzan returns, silver maned in a long
camel coat, *Maggie* she says, shaking his hand—
after the robbing prossie in the song, not Thatcher,

me da had some pride and they both laugh
till it hurts. Lord and Lady Heseltine
are presented with a framed aerial photograph

and a jar of Stockbridge Village honey.

> *Although you have no silver spoon*
> *Better days are coming soon*

Sugar

for Godfrey

Persuaded by hand-tinted postcards
of Buckingham Palace and Trafalgar Square
he left the scratching dogs and chickens
to the baked Trinidadian dirt, made a gift
of his sparkling fish to the girl next-door,
left the mango trees to Green Honeycreepers
and the Oilbirds clicking from their cave ledges,
packed his suitcase on his box-bed
flew towards the glimmer of Wolverhampton
and the Sunbeam cars his father Walter
was to build, was lost in corridors
on his first school day, answered *yes please*
to the teacher who asked would he like the cane,
grinned at the thought of its fibrous sweetness,
held out his hand for the promise.

Bird

He doesn't like her mouth of neat teeth, its yaff,
mistakes his own temper for courage, the careful
placing of a blow as restraint, a skill.

She speaks in one hundred voices,
wears thorn-proof gloves and
like a gardener looks to the ground.

Sleeping with her is like holding a bird,
the soft beat of its frightened heart
in his palm.

In the bath, she studies the life-cycle
of a bruise, its sudden lividness and then
its dull blurred day-to-day darkening.

Sometimes he leaves the window open
and she looks out, the breeze
lifting her feathers.

He spins honey onto a silver spoon
turns it over and over, measures
the sweet weight of it.

Pipe

She kept his pipe, removed his sins
one by one with cotton buds
until her fingers smelt of him.

She cut his hair, snipped
and snipped 'til all there was
was blue-white scalp.

She kept his rings, laced them through
with kitchen string,
hung them round her pretty neck.

She pulled his teeth,
ground them grey between two rocks
and made a paste with vinegar.

She cleaved his fingers
through each knuckle,
chucked them in the biscuit tin.

She closed her eyes,
she heard his voice,
felt its weight upon her bones.

Invisible

He acts as if she were invisible
but lifts his feet when she hoovers.

She sends poems with postal orders
to competitions, but never wins.

He has a locked room of songs
torn from the throats of birds.

She sits on a cold plastic chair while the doctor
scratches the soles of her feet with a hairpin.

He parks his lorry on wasteland
and turns off the engine.

She enjoys astrology and has a moon hat
hidden in the utility room.

He eats his meat first, then pushes
the vegetables around the plate.

She'll tar him one night with a stubby brush,
black him out from head to toe.

Doctor Zeeman's Catastrophe Machine

No more than elastic bands and a wheel
nailed to plywood. My wife rolls her eyes
when the doctor shows how our moods
stretch out, how at a certain point
the slightest shift in the pendulum
can set us spinning.

He draws arrows with a red felt pen
on a sheet of paper, talks about
displacement and its dependency
on the load while he twists it
in his hands.

You're here he says smiling
above the fold
on the cusp of catastrophe
where I've written growl.

Punch and Judy

Uncle Alan told me about my mother as a girl,
how one morning, when no-one else dared
she banged on the door of the man down the street,
called him out still bleary with drink, shamed him
on his own doorstep for the work
his cobblestone fists had done to his wife.

Our boy strode past the cross-legged rows
to the front of the hall, looked up the striped tent
shook his fist and demanded it stop.
This is wrong he said, *this is wrong, it isn't fair*
and everyone laughed. I showed him after
the man loading puppets into their box.

Failure

after Gillian Wearing: 2 into 1

He loves me
I suppose. I am a failure,
there's a better way of doing things.
I am a dramatic woman. I know
I think too much of myself and I should
be submissive—a proper wife.
He's very caring really. He says I like to
be dominated. When he's jealous
he's abusive towards me. I'm afraid I won't
grow old—I sometimes tell him that.
He's beautiful looking. He will
try and tell me about love,
but hate is something he needs
and I don't. He says I am a failure

and I don't. He says I am a failure
but hate is something he needs.
Try and tell me about love.
He's beautiful looking; he will
grow old. I sometimes tell him that
he's abusive towards me. I'm afraid I won't
be dominated when he's jealous.
He's very caring—Really? He says I like to
be submissive—a proper wife.
I think too much of myself and I should.
I am a dramatic woman! I know
there's a better way of doing things.
I suppose I am a failure,
he loves me.

Ears

Ossicles: tiny bones
in their cavernous workshop
knocking noise into shape.

Boxed and pressed between
thumb and forefinger, outside
the headmaster's office.

Hiding in hair, fearful of barbers:
the snipping of scissors, or worse
the sound of the strop.

A man needs large ears
in order to hear the sound
of his own voice.

Aching bowls of pus plugged
with cotton wool, nothing
between them, jugged.

Separated twins, each suspicious
of the other, believing itself
to be doing all the work.

Protruding, pink, curled, chewy
cartilage, convenient for lovers
and torturers alike.

Ears never stop,
continue to bloom
even after death.

Ears

Wet behind your shell-like.
Pin back your cauliflowers.
Music to your lugholes.

Bluebottles in a bell jar,
rebuttals, infant school
recitals, insults, tinnitus.

The bald orator stands
back to the light, unaware
of their red glow.

Sound collects like pollen
in a hollow tunnel,
awaits transmission.

The mucus crackle
of a head cold, the dog's
underwater bark.

Pressed to a glass, pressed
to a wall, hearing
nothing good about itself.

If it were not for the trickle of blood,
it may have been that he'd just lain down
to sleep at the policeman's feet.

Cabin Pressure.
Open-mouthed.
Gulp, blow, pop.

The Difference Engine

The two brothers are the silent
childless keepers of a language.

One sits on a high stool
in white gloves and cranks the handle.

Eight thousand cast iron parts move
and interlock, tooth against tooth.

They go quietly about the task:
the elimination of human error,

the mathematics of family
to thirty one decimal places.

The number wheel presses
calculations into soft plaster.

The second brother
scratches them out.

The Tyran Piano Teaching Machine Mk II

Madame Tyran hisses from the tape, her accent
pitched between Paris and Macclesfield:

C D E F G A B
C D E F G A B

You play like a horse and not a good horse,
a three legged horse, a horse with no sense
of time, a horse whose ugly wife left him
for a ballroom dancer she met at the leisure centre.

'Where is the circle of admiring sophisticates
as pictured in your ad? The leather wrist-straps
pinch like a spiteful girl and the white keys
are smeared with blood from my rattled knuckles.'

Do you hear banging? That is my head and the wall,
try and keep to that rhythm. Is chopsticks so difficult?
Drag me to the woods s'il vous plait, bury me deep beyond sound.

'I do not believe, Madame, that you studied
at the Conservatoire National Supérieur de Musique
nor trust your money back guarantee.'

Perhaps Middle C on your shitty piano is hiding somehow,
is not in plain view above the lock awaiting your stupid thumb.
Let me tighten the neck-brace a notch or two.

'Madame, Madame, please I am quite breathless.
The mechanical arm is going wild with the hairbrush.'

You must learn that art is a struggle monsieur.
I beat it into you: prestissimo, prestissimo!

Double Woodwork

We unfurl our aprons.

I will carve a pair of imploring hands
from a picture in this art magazine sir
and daydream the Renaissance.

The other boys shall chisel dove-tail joints
from four-by-two held in vices, assemble
pencil cases as neat as coffins.

The horizon is technical college
and factories. O Leonardo
I crave fat olives and prosciutto.

And if this stubborn wood continues
to refuse my artistry, why I shall simply
turn my hand to poetry or something.

I will not fall into the machinery
of this town, these hands,
these hands are not made for that.

Grain

A document landed
on a nut-brown table,

you in the hall, a raw face
unwrapped from its scarf.

There'll be a morning
when you let in the light,

a comb through your hair
pulling away loose strands.

Under the trees
mushrooms take shape.

From grain,
bread warm to the table.

How to Make a Family

1. Find a Daddy's girl, bright
as a bell, let her down twice.

A fox's bark cracks open
a quiet suburban night.

2. Let him be no more than a lad,
give him two older sisters.

A metal detectorist digs up a fourth century
bejewelled pennant of a horse.

3. Put them in an office block, give him
the courage to turn back on the stairs.

An actress forgets her lines in the second act
and ad libs something inappropriate.

4. Take him to the top of a ladder,
have him look down.

A teenage girl climbs out from a pothole
after thirty eight hours—live on the evening news.

5. Let them take walks in their lunch breaks,
laminate passes swinging from their necks.

A hybrid delphinium blooms blue
shows its stamens and pistils.

6. Let them try it out for a while
in her parents' spare room.

For one night only, the northern lights
are visible in Middlesborough.

7. Send them off to the ring road
for paint and cheap furniture.

A cowboy falls dead from the saloon roof
in the Sunday afternoon movie.

Knitting Machine

Mother flings back her coat tails,
takes her seat
behind the spindle-legged apparatus.

    surveys the room,
    sets the tension dial,
    waits for silence

and then a sudden clattering swoop
and then another, another, another
like a departing train.

The carpet's laid out
in a strict grid pattern.
My cars set off from their tin garage

at decent intervals, race from crossroad
to crossroad, plastic tyres whirring
on the bright nylon tufts.

We are a wordless song:
    to my skinned knees,
    to her swollen knuckles,
    aching for needles.

The Bonsack Machine

In 1875, the Allan & Ginter company in Richmond, Virginia offered a prize of US $ 75,000 for the invention of a machine able to roll cigarettes. James Albert Bonsack (October 9, 1859 – June 2, 1924) took up the challenge and left school to devote his time to building such a machine.

The boy's head was all cogs
and pulleys, best Virginia sweet with sugar, glycerine
and molasses flowed through his contraption's whirling
blades. It did the work of six hundred Carolina
factory girls, cranked out more perfect white cigarettes
than anyone could sell.

So enter
James Buchanan Duke

Buck Duke:
visionary,
cigar-smoker,
salesman.

Farmers, soldiers in trenches, Mr President,
women in doorways, nervous types and office workers

this is modern, hygienic city-living, untouched
by human hands or spit,

put your pen or spade down,
fetch yourself a cup of Joe, rock back and close
your eyes, picture the cards in your album:

Keokuk, Smoky Joe Wood, Sitting Bull, Home Run
Baker, Rushing Bear, Eddie Plank, Geronimo,

and ladies who's to say you shouldn't know
this pleasure too, light yourself a Torch of Freedom,
march roaring down Fifth Avenue,

keep a slender figure,
so very smooth, so satisfying, so naturally gentle
and so mild.

O the glamour, the glamour,
Hepburn at Tiffany's, Bogart in shadow, hepcats mooched
in cellar bars, autumn ceilings rich with tar, Jean-Paul
Sartre and Gauloises.

Taste me! Taste me! Come on and Taste Me!

that first sweet candy cigarette, masquerade and camaraderie,
the bike shed's sulphur reek, Mr Watson's tête-à-tête,
that burn across your unclenched fist, the shrouded promise
of the grammar schoolgirls upstairs on the bus –

so Round, so Firm, so Fully-Packed, so Free
                    and Easy on the Draw –

in your brother's budgie jacket
underneath the Town Hall clock and in the Odeon's
groping dark – let our exhalations rise up
to the conjuror's one-eyed glare, all
'a la lumiere'

and –

you're never alone with a Strand –

so two's up on that tab and let's hear it for:

knuckled prison currency
cold mornings
ground out underfoot
     the spit
of tobacco on your tongue,
nicotine stains and lemon juice,
push-button ashtrays,
veiled lounges and fusted yawns,
the breathless stairs
and something to look forward to
after sex,

always milder, better tasting, cooler smoking,
what your doctor recommends –

and now you'll find us philosophising
in designated smoking areas, lying
with our shadowed lungs, 'aving a fag
from Madison Avenue, to Beasley Street.

Fixed

My father gave me a Delmonta
twin lens reflex. A German camera
from the Fifties.

Everything's murky on the ground glass
and moving in the opposite direction
to what you'd expect.

My new mother loves the camera
and it loves her back. She holds baking
straight from the oven under its nose;

laughs for it when she's drinking
and smoking; blows it kisses; parades
each new dress for it; closes her

beautiful mascara eyes and sleeps
for it. I conjure her in the darkroom,
wash away the silver, fix her, make her permanent.

Camera

is an eye
as a mouth

is sprung blades
snapping shut

is your dad
in a suit

is prepared
to lie

is full
of regrets

is better behaved
on Sundays

is an empty bed
in a room

is carefully placed
is elsewhere

is proof
of the loss

School Room, Upper Silesia 1933

Freedom and Bread

In that moment when the shutter was pressed
no-one looked away. So the camera
held each luminous face in its gaze, kept
them there, each grin, lost look or open stare.

Fifty boys in rows, with folded arms or hands
in front, their grubby fingers curling over
the rims of wooden desks. The master stands
at the back, his hat on a peg by the door.

He tells them that knowledge is wealth.
My father looks out from the third row
chin raised and clear-eyed, sure of himself,
but there were things he couldn't know.

The alphabet hangs on the wall, every
underlined letter chanted until known
well enough for words to come easy,
as beyond the door, the first stones are thrown.

One boy blinked and is given clouds for eyes.
The smallest sits at the front and wears
a dirty striped jacket, his face betrays
that he already knows the use of words.

The words on the streets are Fire and Murder
they ring clear against the tenement blocks
and shop windows. The schoolmaster
turns the key of a black music box,

its wooden bird rises from her burning nest
a voice as pure as the serious child -
black tie and leather strap across his chest
which rises and falls where his heart is held

and beats quietly in a bed of soft ash.
Its slow grey storm coats tongues, clogs nostrils
and stings eyes. By the time they can wash,
scrape it away from under their fingernails,

they'll have become men of sorts, outgrown
the classroom's hard benches and made their way;
some in polished boots, some with triangles sewn
on their shirts and nothing left to know.

The Machine Gun

After Stephen Graham 'A Private in the Guards' (1919)

The machine gun
is designed
to fire

continuously
when the trigger's
held down;

can reduce a man
tangled in the wire
to rags;

has an open bolt
to permit cooling
between bursts.

Beloved

Luzi addressed him in his own language,
Mein geliebter schatz and like a schoolgirl
drew a biro heart around *Ich Liebe Dich.*

This time he doesn't need to cross the Alps
in war-time to reach his sweetheart, he kneels
before her in Debenhams and places slippers

on her tiny feet. She takes him home
and his German returns with no trace
of an accent, his army pension restored.

Letters are full of how much better
everything is there. *The best doctors in the world*
sent them, free, to a Bavarian Spa.

They take slow walks amongst the pines.
Son the air is so clear you can see for miles.
You must all come over in the Audi.

Bring:

Yorkshire tea-bags,
Marks and Spencer's beige 42 inch stretch waist Crimplene slacks,
Boots' own brand constipation relief tablets.

They emerge from their chalet
like the kissing couple from a cuckoo clock,
greet us in a muddle of German and English.

Reservoir

After a century of quiet work, the reservoir
found a way into the subterranean darkness,
rushed down the fell in less than an hour
and went. The church spire broke the surface,
a bracelet of row-boats hung from the car park.
On the crag, the ruined castle windows wept
for choked machinery, for kittens in sacks
and the school's forgotten alphabet.

The early hiker tried hard to fathom the blue
of his map, villagers climbed bleary-eyed
from bath-like beds, peered through
curtains at the road's sudden bright blade,
stumbled into kitchens of brimming pans
and out of back doors to wring their hands.

Coat

Give me your tobacco coat
and black hat father. Sink
into the cracked leather chair.

Let's have a good look at you:
your white shins and loose teeth,
your monkish bald patch.

Let's go through the albums,
those ridiculous poses.
Who's this and this?

Your hands seem a little shaky old man,
be careful with your tea.
Tell me the truth this time.

We can take it to the scrubby end
of the garden, to the sodden leaves,
look out across that stubbled field.

Mechanical Turk

Chess Playing Machine 1770-1854

I am a learned man
reduced to nothing more
than a magic trick
folded inside this box.

I am flickering shadows.
I am smirched by candle smoke and sweat.
I am a speaker of languages
who must hold his tongue.

> Your Majesty, ladies and gentlemen I am
> Wolfgang Von Kempelen and I present
> to you: The Turk, an Oriental wonder.
>
> This is no trick, no illusion, no sleight
> of hand. No matter which door you open,
> only mechanical workings.
>
> And see,
> the Turk himself: no beating heart,
> just cogs and levers.
>
> Sceptics, please come nearer
> and inspect the machine,
> place your lodestones as close as you wish.

This is how it works:
I make my moves in the choking gloom
and the Turk's metal arm
creakily does my bidding
in the palace's glittered light.

The people are enchanted, eyes agog
as their King is toppled.

The Turk's clockwork tongue whirs,
issues his oath: *échec échec échec.*

Father's Diary

She's reading her father from cover to cover.
He harks at the listening,

jabs the fire with a poker
whilst she scatters on pages.

He tips coal from the scuttle,
vanishes in a black cloud,

reappears like a minstrel
flashing his terrible eyes and teeth.

On the way out, he leaves prints
by the light switch; turns on the dark.

Blink

The blink and ozone stench
Of the photocopier

A tempered window
Blank with sugar paper

A skewed snapshot
Held with a pin

The claw and drag
Of the wireless mouse

A corridor of doors
Dark with varnish

A tangle of cables
And the recycling box

A fluorescent tube's sour light
Soaking up the evening

Archived accounts
In a locked cabinet

The Machinery of Government

is turned by an ox, hooves clumping
through its own golden circle of dung.

We beetles are guided by milky stars,
scarab backs gleaming in celestial light.

We are all dwellers, rollers or tunnellers.
This is what we live for.

Spring

Snow keeps falling though April's begun. The city
is buried while we sleep in our beds
and the council's run out of molasses and grit.

People move through the streets like hospital patients
out for a smoke or a breath of fresh air,
the onset of chilblains cracking their skin.

The park is bereft of hopeful spring tulips
and so are the verges and vases on sideboards.
There's just enough power for a couple more weeks.

What then? We'll start to burn tables and chairs
I suppose. A family in crampons takes the road into town
for what tins are left on the shelves in the shops.

Their faces are stung by the wind from the lake
where anglers in pin-stripes crouch over the ice
watching the city the other way up.

The King James Version

The night's snow hit him in the face
as he struggled up the steps, where
as a younger man, with one blow,
he'd felled a trouble-maker before
he could reach the pub door.

He set off down the lane,
focused on the glittering at his feet,
wide forester's shoulders covered
by a dark coat. He was a shape
cut from the blizzard. It's thought

he'd been a scholar. Between pinches
of snuff he'll quote the bible and give
the dates of battles, name the apostles
in alphabetical order for a pint of beer.

The snow covered him as he slept.
The common view is that the alcohol
saved him, although science says
he should have died all the more quickly.

Who knows then, how he woke
in the morning, shook the snow
from his coat, startling the bus queue
before clearing his throat and proclaiming:

> *I am the resurrection, and the life:*
> *he that believeth in me, though*
> *he were dead, yet shall he live.*
> *John: Chapter 11, Verse 25.*

They gaped through the bus's filthy windows
like fish, as he slouched towards home.

Sensing Space

after Li Xiaodong

The walls are a passing train,
each bound upright stick
an episode from your life in Braille.

       The sweet beech smell of window ledges;
       a knock – knock joke; a Clash t-shirt
       peeled from an acned back; spit and love.

Stood on brittle aggregate; the horizon
a mirror. The gilded sky looses its rain,
the stones darken for a while.

       A margarita's kick; the book's
       cracked spine; a gun-grey splinter
       under your skin; next door's music.

Blindfold yourself; rely on squeaks
and sonar like a bat. Press palm to palm
against the cool glass.

       Grief; diesel on your gloves; the creak
       and heave of a sudden shift
       in the machinery.

Remove your shoes and socks; walk barefoot
through the curtain. Don't try to return
for what you've forgotten.

Sparrows

Two Years to Retirement
Two Years to Retirement
covers the required time-span
for each repetition of the stretch
prescribed by the physiotherapist.

My muscles unknot like a tie.
I turn from spreadsheet cells
to reach for the walls, gaze
through the small window
to where gable meets gable.

The roof catches the late light,
but other than that
there's usually nothing to see.

Only today
there's a few buffish sparrows
jostling to slide down the gutter
then hop back
for another go.

Have they not the whole sky?
Are there no twigs to gather,
no gaping yellow beaks
chirping hungrily in nests?
Or perhaps, for today
the worms can wait.

Reservist

The fusted kit bag, *Two Four Two Seven*
Double Two Three Four Private Figura
in cracked white paint on its flank,
drops from the attic, stands upright
for a moment before the kick of gravity
sends it down the stairs to lie prone
on the hall carpet. The reek of gun-oil,
knees and elbows scuffed by chalky
South Downs grit, a white patch
pasted to a plywood man's chest,
the thin-lipped Captain's command,
the crack to cheekbone as the shock
echoes back and the pitted sand dances.

Sciatica

for Yanny Mac

Our code word is *Pilates*
we take short careful steps and never go
too far, for fear of the whip
to buttocks, the backs of our legs.

You'll find us watching
from the edge of the dance floor
on large blue inflatable balls,
our backs pressed to the radiators.

We know the proper cost of a dropped
coin, the love and hate
of the masseur's knuckles
and not to fill the fridge's lower shelves.

During the sexual act we tightrope walk
the line between pleasure and pain, let out
small cries and yelps that are often mistaken
for encouragement. Some people
would pay good money for this.

We're not short of contradictory advice,
watch the top three exercises
for herniated discs on a loop
on YouTube. We owe our souls to Pfizer
and must not operate machinery.

Cross-sectioned on the screen
like a side of pork, at each vertebrae
a pair of meaty chops. We wince
when our shadows are tapped
with the point of a pen.

There's a doctor in the old town
who'll plunge you in ice, then strap you
greased up and naked to a spinning table
and fire electricity through your bones
for a hundred quid.

We're badly played banjos, we recognise
each others' tune, huddle together
on low walls or benches, swop rumours
about those who've calmed this nerve,
got themselves back.

Life Support Machine

They've called it a coma
though his thousand yard stare
makes it look like a trance

and his eyes are eclipses
a thin fringe of blue
flaring the outer space

dark of his pupils
and his friends can't help
tapping their feet

to the beep beep beep
Balearic Beat
of the life support machine.

Blinds all drawn
the Day-Glo green
ghosts the hooded dark.

When the drugs kick in
he picks up the groove
at first no more

than a spasm or a twitch
then his hands
chop shapes from the air.

And when they drop
he's a smile on his face
as the line falls flat on the screen.

Washing Machine

To you whitest of white goods, usurper
of wash-board, dolly peg and mangled
drudgery, autumn sale ring road retail
outlet item, steel drum beating kitchen
dancer, dry-clean only label chancer,
loose change rattling money launderer,
lonely housewife hotpoint pleaser, YES
YES YES you fast-spin Cyclops, bless
you father stain absolver, shocking
pink white shirt disaster, Omo
-sapien bobby dazzler, blue pullover
pulveriser, student's stinking hold
-all holding moaning mother
emphathiser, laundrette punter
mesmeriser, sodding suddy slick
floor-flooder, magic trick odd sock
provider, old grey knicker elastic
stretcher, butcher's apron cold-blood
-letter, man-sized tissue snow globe
shaker, filth and dirt disintegrator,
radiator damp wool feeder, Levi Strauss
blue denim fader, duvet cover
and bed sheet wrangler, ambassador
for washing powder, juddering
goggle-eyed basement beast.

Nissan

The little silver Nissan smells of them:

bay rum and lavender,
the National Trust's *Fifty Best Woodland Walks*,
an out of date road atlas,
boiled sweets and arguments,
a swinging pine tree,
driving gloves,
a tow-rope,
picnic blanket,
an emergency shovel.

Cloth

She throws the cloth over the small table,
watches it billow and settle, then smooths
it out corner to corner, palms singing.

She admires its perfect circle and lace edge,
its glow, berths the salt and pepper pots
in their little boat next to the ketchup.

He'll loosen his tie in a moment
and say something nice about the fish.
She watches him reach for the water jug.

She shakes the cloth from the kitchen door,
scatters crumbs onto the crazy paving
for the greedy little sparrows to peck at.

A Martin Sends a Postcard Home

after Craig Raine

They wear green suits with many sleeves,
and measure out bright-liquids

that tighten your eyes, render your tongue
too heavy to lift. Pretty boy, pretty boy

hangs from a tinkling dome admiring
his mimic. Desert winds blur the view

to red felt. The grey contraption
in my head-case is softening, the past

is pinned faces, including my own
blowing a kiss to seventy dripping flames.

Rust is mortality in the form of a cloak,
ice a lock of water, like spring wrapped

in tissue paper. Each afternoon
music is played from cylinders

and their arms become snakes.
The moving window in the corner

is silenced for a while. Time is upside down
until someone holds your wrist and counts.

Days here are stretched as thin
as a balloon. The iron mouth

in my room hides my treasures. Its teeth
are sequenced to the date of my birth.

I have it written down somewhere. Last week
they took us out in rows of chairs.

The cake tasted of sulphur
and the cheap memories I bought

fall off the big white box
where the cold is kept. Their old

are revered and put in Kilner jars
on the shores of empty lakes.

They drink terrible tea through one
of their mouths and try to touch our hair.

Yesterday someone I didn't know
came to visit - was it you?

From where I'm sitting
the Earth looks like your pockmarked face.

Mrs Smith

It's true, I sometimes sit on the floor
to smoke a cigarette while the enamel bath fills.

My daughters tower above me
and the washing line is never empty.

I know the thinness of my daughters' skin,
have their little house of secrets in my palm.

What will we do with all these rooms? One day
they'll gather around my raised-up bed.

I've grasped freckled forearms, walked backwards
through the blue shallow end of the municipal pool.

Once we swam in Loch Leven, our white limbs
in the dark water, their father watching from an island.

Tree Shaking Machine

He lurches up the grove
like some film dell'orrore beast:
half lobster, half bat.

I offer a trembling branch
he grabs my throat
and shakes.

All my piccoli bambini
fall into the darkness
of his thrown cloak.

And what can I do
but wave in the breeze
and pray to Madonna:

      be they not be pitted
      and jarred in brine,

      be they not be pressed
      to lampante or pomace,

      be they not drowned
      in vermouth for a lush,

      lie them with pomodoro and mozzarella
      on a bright maiolica plate,

      raise a simple chianti
      to the sunshine and smile.

Anaesthesia and The Sea That Has Become Known

I have held her heart in my hand and it's fine; you are good people.
Surgeon, Great Ormond Street Hospital

Sweet curmudgeon
Moon-faced child
Moon at the top of the stairs
Cheese thief and comical saint

Sternum split like wood
His open palm
Its line of fortune
Your yarn-stitched heart

Your hands of fire
Their Simian Crease
Cuttlebone Moon
Masked Moon
Moon adrift
The hauled up ladder
A dinosaur spine

Sea of Vapors
Serpent Sea
Sea of Crises
Ocean of Storms
Sea of Cold
Sea that has become known

Come on home
Sliver of moon
Wild-eyed moon
Rattle of stones
Moon of rain
Moon of love

We're good people
Glimmer of Moon
And you're our Moon
Shine down Moon
As though nothing
Were amiss

Amy's Lovers

It's not enough to love them,
she must climb into their skins
and wear them like pyjamas.

It's Fireman Sam just now, has been
for a couple of years. She wanders
that pyromaniacal valley town

with matches in her back-pack.
She'll smoke out the hero
inside herself, hits rewind again

and again, can't get enough
of his tune or his merchandise.
It's as if Springfield never happened

until six pm, when she turns Sam off
for Channel 4, taps her fingertips together
and is Mister Charles Montgomery Burns.

She has his shaky walk down pat
and mimics his villainous laugh,
while Sam pretends to polish his axe.

He knows it's not the last Lothario though,
but the next, some new kid, all pixels,
on the big screen at the multiplex.

A cheap toy with her Big Mac, then
its shopping for DVDs, utility belts
and action figures and his heart's a stone.

Out west, Woody tips back his hat
squints through the haze of all the years
since Shaggy turned up in his mystery machine

and she began to dress in brown
and green and left her sheriff badge
to tarnish. But Woody was first

and best and bides his time.
Toy Stories Two and Three went by,
but he's pretty sure when Four comes out,

she'll mosey into town wearing her cowskin waistcoat,
shout: *Yee-Haw Woody*
as if she's never been gone.

Amy's Calendar

You clutch my forearm, little white bear,
a pinch of skin in your fist. The house
is tiptoe quiet, the fight surrendered
to gripe water and charcoal. I dare
not move, but for the rise and fall
of my belly. I'm tethered by a fingertip
to the insistent tug of your mouth,
the extra chromosome of your map.

You drift off to a house of picture charts
with Velcro symbols for household chores
and activities. You have your own calendar,
enjoy Hoovering and bowling most of all.
Every Tuesday you must have the same sandwich
from Subway or the moon will fall from the sky.
I am a stick man, my dates clearly marked,
yet somehow, I am ill-prepared.

Difference Engine No2

In a family there are relationships at play,
a measurable space between values.

What is a norm?

The orbital limits of members may differ widely
making comparisons unstable. This is often the case
when the dynamics of it are chaotic.

By studying the trajectory of one member
difficulties arise. Some may wander erratically,
become lost or vulnerable like a free spinning wheel
coupled to a small motor by a spring.

The behaviour of one affects the behaviour
of others, biology and magic have a role to play.

It may well separate into two parts: one that converges
towards the orbit, another that diverges from the orbit.

An equation is an equality; an interdependency
is not necessarily true or known. The parameters
of the system may not be identified precisely or terms
may be missing. Some are too complicated to be understood.

A circle map may be used to study the behaviour
of a beating heart, the position and value of a body.

Families are like:
the flow of water in a pipe,
the swing of a pendulum,
the number of fish, each springtime
in a lake.

*The poem has adapted mathematical terms from Wikipedia in turn sourced from texts
by authors including: Andrey Kolmogorov, Mikhail Gromov, Felix Hausdorff and
Glenn James. Mathematical accuracy has been sacrificed to metaphor.*

Light

After Stephen Shore

   there isn't much light
coming off
Davey's motel sign

   rain has left
the place
despondent

   all the words
riding the telephone line
are headed out of town

   the window
is nothing
but white light

   a battered
grey Chevvy
skims by

   the bar-maid's
dress
is colour-blind

   a knife edge
bides
its time

   some young guy
courts a sulky girl
idly pushes

        a line
of spilt sugar
into a heart shape

        something
inside of her
catches light

New Year Redux

Each guest slips from fog
and through the door
like a softly lit movie star

and casts adrift: the new-build houses
opposite, the call centres, the inner ring-road's
constant hum and this little room

is warm and bright with party dresses
and men with quiffs in baggy suits
and in the bedroom up above

where all the faux-fur coats
are chucked, the radio's clock flips back
and back and above the roof, above the fog

stars are streaks across the sky
and above all that, beehives glow
like standard lamps and Louis Prima swings

and jokes are spilt and someone shouts
fetch me a blowsy woman now
and his wife throws her scarf

about his neck, kisses him loose
upon the mouth and from our mouths
If you knew Susie, like I know Susie

Oh, Oh, Oh, what a girl and in the yard
fog is smoke and smoke is breath
and cigarettes are shooting stars

and through the misted window's blur
is that my mother's gap-toothed grin,
my aunts and uncles counting down

and is this me at the back door
a lump of coal gripped in my fist?

To a Grey Seal

Not a sparkling turquoise sea—murk,
each low swell a tip-toe exultation
until there's a knife at my throat.

The sea creels your theremin cry
from somewhere north
as I'm lifted clear by the drag.

I can't see even my own pale feet,
they must be in the gloom with my ankles
and shins; my two-legged clumsiness.

You come close, my whiskery sea-pig
with your black polished eyes, give me
your best bright stenchy yawn.

I hope you haven't dreamt me as threat
(surely not), or fish, my shriven fruit
some treat, an amuse-bouche?

And you're quick and gone, the sea blank
to the horizon's wind turbines,
to the reclaimed lowlands of Europe.

The thrill of a rough bump to my thigh
has my heart ragged at my ribs. I've heard tell
of sex-starved males dragging a soul

under the waves. And another bump,
then another, before you surface
innocent and curious as Sunday's child.

Is it a game you want, or perhaps to guide me
to where my skin waits sloughed on the cloudy bed
so I might return to the islands.

But I've a wife on the shore with my towel
and the key to our little caravan
on a length of string. Tonight, over wine

as the sun slips low and gold
I'll tell her again and again
how far out I was, and how wild.

Waxham Sands

fold me into your dun coat
of grasswort and cord grass,

let my ribs become
a small wrecked boat.